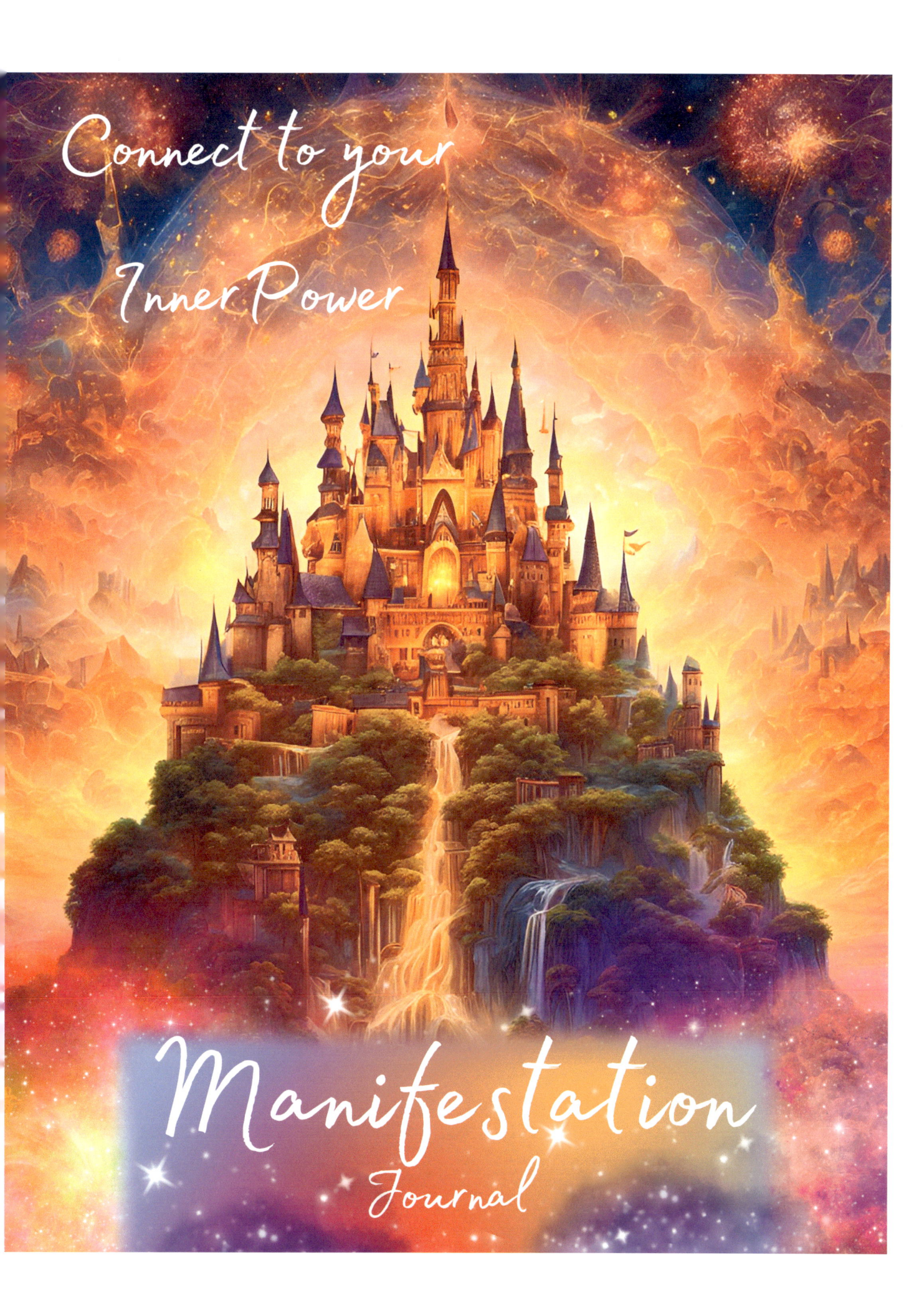

Connect to your
Inner Power

Manifestation
Journal

"Remember Magic Starts within,
and YOU can be your most powerful tool."

Envisioned By
Freyja Seithr

ai generated images

Let's Start with Purpose

The purpose of this Journal is to teach you how to align yourself with the frequency of the universe, making your manifestations more effective and enhancing your inner power.

Aligning with the universe's frequency is based on the ancient idea that everything in the universe, including thoughts and emotions, colors, crystals, herbs, and certain archetypes, vibrate at a specific frequency.

Here's how this concept is thought to help manifest dreams:

1. Resonance and Attraction: When you align your frequency (through your thoughts, feelings tools, and actions) with what you desire, you create a resonance that attracts similar energies and opportunities. This is similar to the well known Law of Attraction, where like attracts like. When you use certain tools you can attract a specific frequency.

2. Positive Mindset: Focusing on positive thoughts and emotions raises your frequency. This positive mindset can enhance your confidence, motivation, and overall well-being, making it easier to pursue and achieve your goals.

3. Clarity and Intention: Being clear about what you want and setting strong, specific intentions can help align your frequency with your desires. This clarity acts as a powerful signal to the universe, guiding your actions and attracting corresponding opportunities.

4. Emotional Alignment: Emotions play a crucial role in frequency alignment. Feeling gratitude, joy, and excitement about your dreams, even before they manifest, can align your energy with the frequency of those dreams, helping to draw them into reality.

Let's Start with Purpose

5. Mindfulness and Presence: Practices like meditation, visualization, and mindfulness help tune your frequency by bringing your mind into a state of calm and focus. This alignment with the present moment enhances your ability to manifest by reducing resistance and increasing flow.

6. Taking Inspired Action: Aligning with the universe's frequency isn't just about thoughts and feelings; it also involves taking action. When you are in alignment, you are more likely to recognize and seize opportunities, make decisions that support your goals, and stay committed to your path.

In essence, aligning with the universe's frequency means harmonizing your thoughts, emotions, and actions with your desires. This holistic approach can create a powerful synergy that helps manifest your dreams into reality.

How to use this Journal

At the start of this Journal, you will learn about the ancient concept of using specific tools to attract a specific frequency on a daily basis to align you with the universe. When I say the universe, I am referring to the source that flows through all life and teaching you how to harness that source by becoming one with ALL that IS.

Once you learn and gather the tools you have around you, use this Journal as a guide to creating your own kingdom. We are the masters of our own universe. There is no need to seek for answers outside of self. Once you have the knowledge and tools, you can begin your journey towards your dreams.

Manifestation does not happen without action. Words without works are worthless. It takes dedication and consistency to create the world you dream of. Leave your programming out of this space, and believe that magic is real. It is not "demonic" as some would love for you to believe, it is of the universe and you are the universe, you just need to remember who you are. Your purpose is to awaken your inner power by connecting to the universe on a vibrational level in order to awaken your most authentic self.

Cleanliness is Crucial when Manifesting

Here are the 5 reasons why it's important to clean your space before conducting your metaphysical workings to manifest your dreams.

1. Purity and Focus: Cleanliness helps maintain purity in your practice, ensuring that your intentions and energy are not contaminated by residual or negative energies. A clean space promotes clarity and focus, which are essential for effective workings.

2. Respect for the Practice: Keeping your tools and space clean demonstrates respect for the magical practice and the entities or forces you might be working with. It shows dedication and reverence, which can enhance the effectiveness of your work.

3. Symbolic Fresh Start: Cleaning your space and tools can symbolize a fresh start, helping to clear away old energies and make room for new intentions. It helps to create an environment conducive to new, positive outcomes and opening new doors to your desired future .

4. Dark/Negative energies thrive in filth: Make sure you clean your space and don't skip the corners - After thoroughly cleaning your space - open the windows and doors and consider using tools such as sage, palo santo, incense, florida water, salt, holy water or crystals to help attract the frequency of clean purified energy and send away any energies that are not aligned with your intentions. If you don't have access to these tools or resources to buy them or make them simply remember that Magic starts within and you can be your most powerful tool .

Cleanliness is Crucial when Manifesting

    5. Improved Energy Flow: A clean and organized space can improve the flow of energy, which is crucial for successful manifestation. Clutter and dirt can obstruct and disrupt the flow of energy, potentially hindering your efforts.

Overall, cleanliness helps ensure that your work is conducted in a pure, respectful, and effective manner leading to enhanced manifestations. There is a reason behind the famous saying, "Cleanliness is next to Godliness".

Clean your Vessel

Eating clean and living a clean lifestyle can significantly enhance your manifesting in several ways:

1. Enhanced Energy and Vitality: Consuming nutritious, unprocessed foods provides your body with the essential nutrients it needs, leading to increased energy levels and overall vitality. A well-nourished body supports clearer thinking and sustained focus, which are crucial for effective manifestation.

2. Mental Clarity: A clean diet and lifestyle help reduce the intake of substances that can cloud the mind, such as excessive sugars, caffeine, and artificial additives. A clear mind improves concentration, intuition, and the ability to set and maintain intentions during your metaphysical practices.

Clean your Vessel

3. Balanced Emotions: Clean living often includes practices such as regular exercise, sufficient sleep, and stress management techniques. These practices help maintain emotional balance and stability, allowing you to approach your manifestations with a calm and focused mindset, free from excessive emotional turmoil.

4. Stronger Connection to Nature: Eating clean often involves consuming whole, natural foods, which can foster a stronger connection to nature. This connection can deepen your understanding and appreciation of natural cycles and energies, enhancing your manifestations and even making enhancing your nature intuitive powers.

5. Physical and Spiritual Purity: A clean lifestyle, free from harmful substances and toxins, promotes physical and spiritual purity. This state of purity can help align your physical body with your spiritual goals, creating a harmonious environment for successful manifestations.

6. Increased Sensitivity: A clean diet and lifestyle can heighten your sensitivity to subtle energies and vibrations. This increased sensitivity can improve your ability to perceive and work with the energies involved in your manifesting. In summary, eating clean and living a clean lifestyle support your manifestations by enhancing your physical, mental, and emotional well-being, fostering a deeper connection to nature, and increasing your sensitivity to subtle energies. This increased sensitivity can help you explore the realms of astral projection much easier as well.

Invoke the Frequency of Monday

The concept of aligning oneself with the "frequency of Monday" stems from ancient astrological and magical traditions where each day of the week is associated with a particular planetary influence. In this context, Monday is linked to the Moon. Here's how you can align yourself with this frequency to assist in your metaphysical workings making your manifestations more effective.

Monday Key

Planetary Influence: The Moon
Attributes: Emotions, intuition, dreams, psychic abilities, femininity, and nurturing.
Frequency: 96hz
Numerology association: No. 2
Element: Water
Colors: Silver, white, pale blue, pearl
Crystals: Moonstone, selenite, pearl
Metal: Silver
Herbs: Jasmine, chamomile, sandalwood, willow, lemon balm, sage, mugwort,
Animals: Horse, stag, bear, raven, deer, minotaur
Chakra: Third eye

Invoke the Frequency of Monday

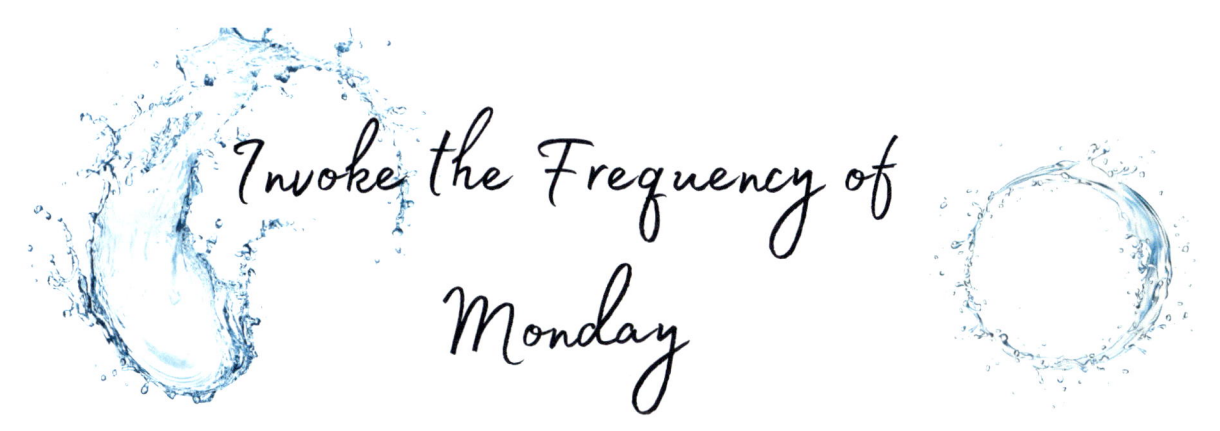

Meditation and Reflection: Spend time in meditation, focusing on your emotions and intuitive thoughts. Practice mindfulness and reflect on your dreams and inner feelings. Recite affirmations to increase your psychic ability or bring stability to your emotions.

Lunar Rituals: Perform prayers or spells that are focused on intuition, emotional healing, and psychic abilities. Conduct these rituals during the evening or night, when the Moon's influence is stronger.

Astrological Timing: Plan your manifestations for Monday to align with the Moon's influence. Pay attention to the lunar phases, as different phases can amplify specific aspects of your workings (e.g., new moons for new beginnings, full moons for manifestation and completion).

Engage with the water element by spending time near bodies of water or incorporating water into your rituals. - Take ritual baths infused with lunar herbs or oils to cleanse and attune yourself to lunar energies. Incorporate the colors silver, white, and pale blue into your environment or clothing. Use lunar symbols like crescent moons in your personal space. Work with crystals like moonstone, selenite, or pearl, carrying them with you or using them in your metaphysical practices. Meditate while holding these crystals to enhance your connection with lunar energies. Burn herbs like jasmine, chamomile, or sandalwood as incense during your practices. Create herbal teas or sachets using these herbs to draw in lunar energy. By incorporating these practices, in connection with your manifestations you can enhance your inner power by aligning with the nurturing and intuitive energies associated with Monday and the Moon.

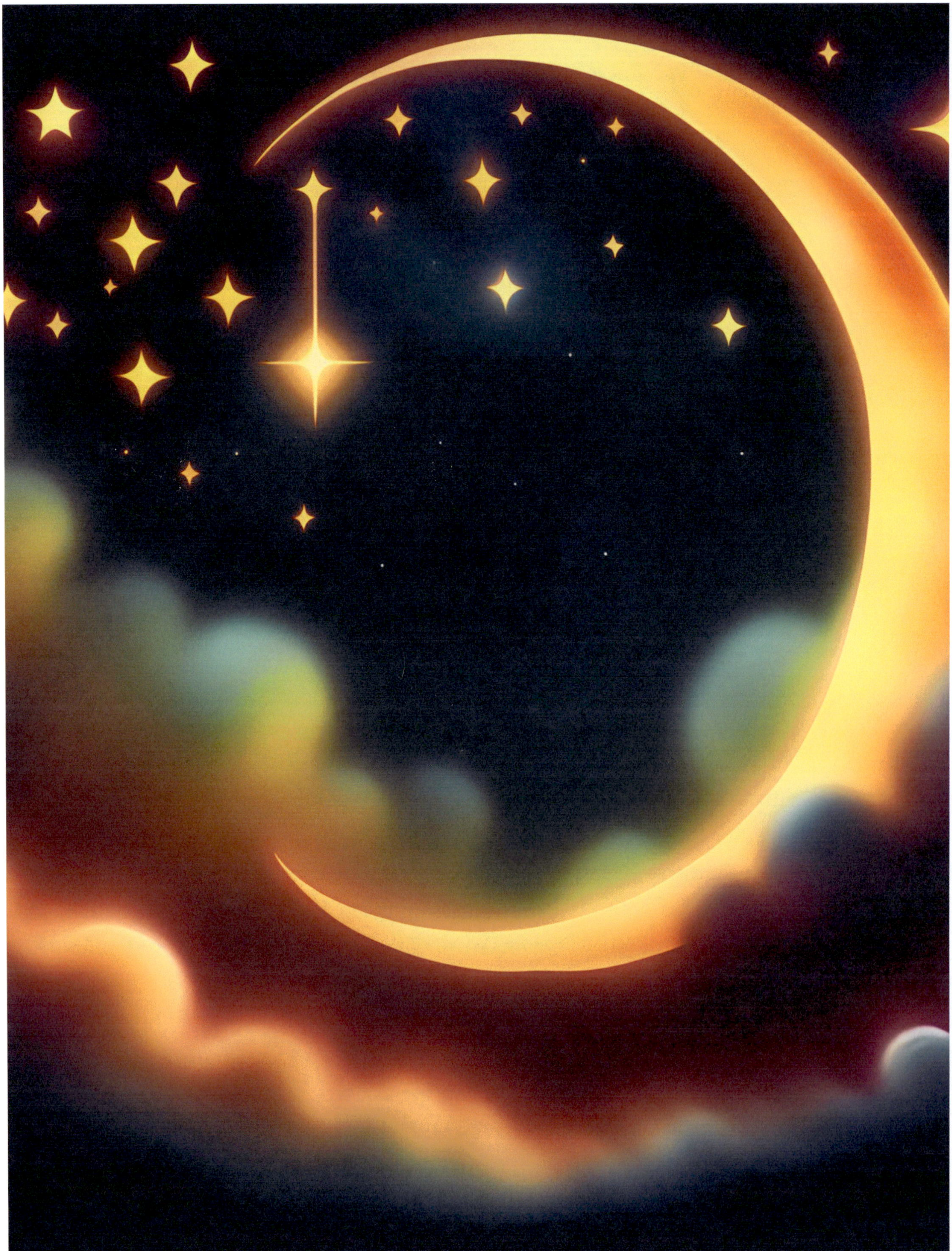

Invoke the Frequency of Tuesday

The frequency of Tuesday is traditionally associated with the planet Mars, which symbolizes energy, drive, courage, and action. In various ancient traditions, aligning oneself with the energy of Tuesday can enhance activities that require assertiveness, determination, and quick action. To align yourself with the frequency of Tuesday and harness this energy set your intentions by Clearly defining your goals and manifestations.

Tuesday Key

Planetary Influence: Mars
Attributes: Raw energy, motivation, action, courage, assertiveness, leadership, aggression, conflict, competition, physical prowess, independence, self-reliance, primal instinct
Frequency: 1152hz
Numerology association: No. 9
Element: Fire
Colors: Red & Burgundy
Crystals/Minerals: Red Coral, red jasper, garnet, ruby
Metal: Iron
Herbs: Bergamot, cinnamon, basil, ginger, nettle
Animals: Wolf, scorpion, werewolf, ram
Chakra: Root

Invoke the Frequency of Tuesday

Aligning your energy with the frequency of Tuesday, a day ruled by Mars, involves tuning into its dynamic, assertive, and action-oriented qualities. Here's how you can align your frequency to the energy of Tuesday making your manifestations more effective and enhancing your inner power. Clearly define what you want to achieve on Tuesday. This might involve setting goals that require assertiveness, courage, and decisive action.

Wear and Use Red: Red is the color most associated with Mars. Wear red clothing or accessories, and incorporate red elements into your workspace or environment to invoke Mars' energy.

Physical Activity: Engage in exercise or physical activities. Mars governs physical vitality and stamina, so activities like running, weightlifting, or even a brisk walk can help you connect with this energy.

Affirmations and Mantras: Use affirmations that resonate with Mars' qualities, such as "I am strong and courageous," "I take decisive action," or "I am filled with energy and drive..

Meditation & Focus: Light a red candle and meditate on your goals. Visualize yourself achieving them with the strength and determination of Mars.

Mars-Related Crystals & Herbs: Use crystals associated with Mars, such as bloodstone, red jasper, or garnet. Carry them with you or place them in your workspace. Burn incense or use herbs associated with Mars, such as basil, ginger, or cinnamon. These can help invoke the planet's energy.

Invoke the Frequency of Tuesday

You might visualize the planet Mars or imagine yourself embodying its attributes of strength, courage, and determination. By incorporating these practices into your Tuesday routine, you can align your energy with the frequency of Mars, enhancing your ability to take decisive actions and achieve your manifestations with assertiveness and vitality.

Invoke the Frequency of Wednesday

In various traditions, Wednesday is associated with different deities, planets, and energies, each of which can influence the day's magical correspondences. Here's an overview of the frequency of Wednesday and how you can align yourself with it, to enhance your manifestation power. Wednesday is associated with Mercury, the planet of communication, intellect, and travel. The energy of Mercury is swift, adaptable, and clever. Mercury is represented by the element of Air, which is connected to thought, communication, and the mind

Wednesday Key

Planetary Influence: Mercury
Attributes: Knowledgeable, lucky, truth, intelligent conversation
Frequency: 216hz
Numerology association: No. 5
Element: Air
Colors: Green, apricot, orange, yellow, purple
Crystals/Minerals: Fire opal, carnelian, aluminum
Metal: Mercury
Herbs: Star anise, fennel, bergamot
Animals: Fox, cheetah, zebra, baboon
Chakra: Sacral

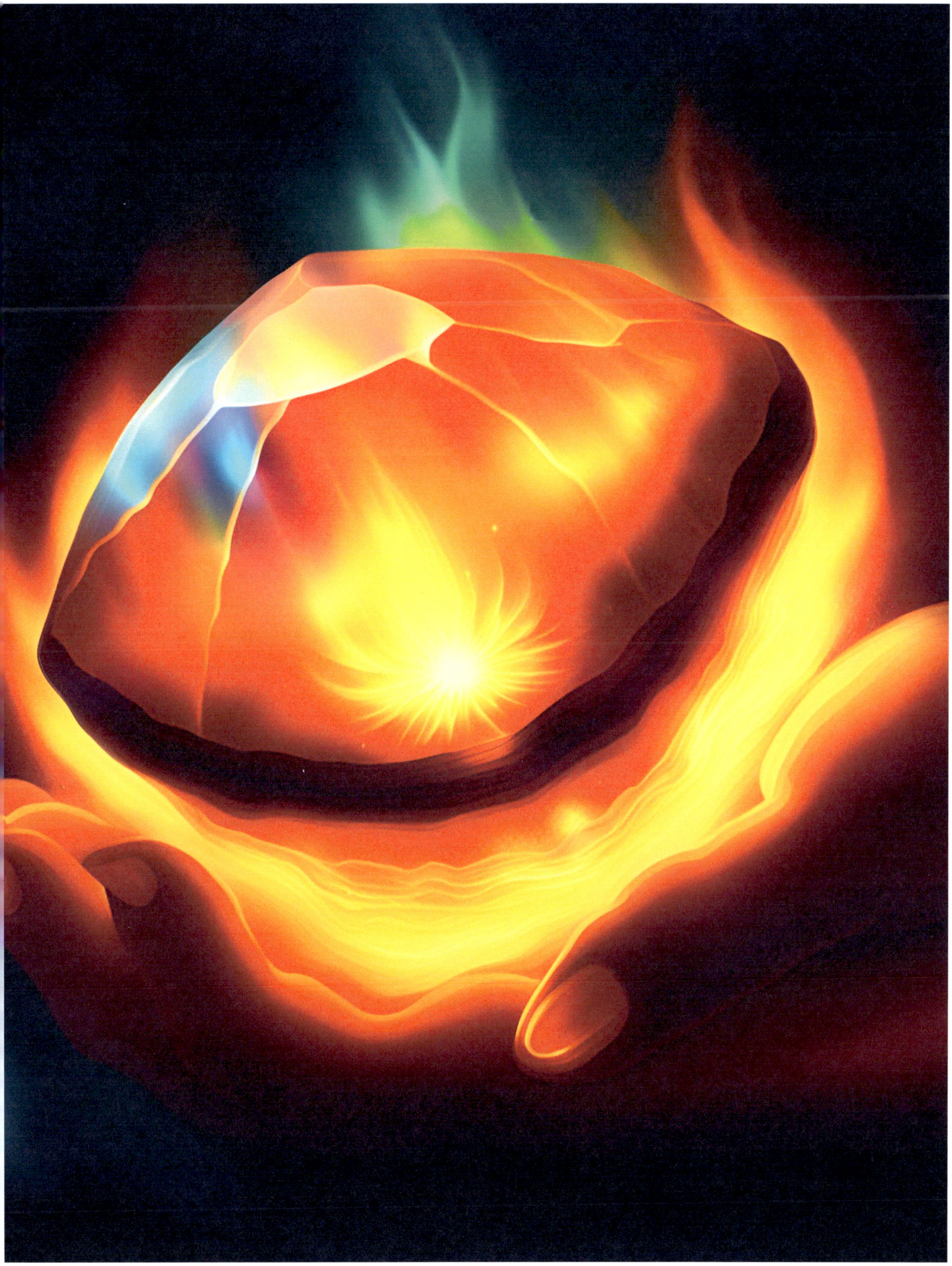

Invoke the Frequency of Wednesday

Deities: Hermes (Greek): The messenger god, patron of commerce, communication, and cunning. Mercury (Roman): Similar to Hermes, representing swiftness, eloquence, and trickery. Odin (Norse): The day's name, "Wednesday," comes from "Woden's day," with Odin being a god of wisdom, war, and magic.

. Meditation and Visualization: Spend time meditating on your goals related to communication, learning, and intellect. Visualize Mercury or your chosen deity guiding you.

Affirmations: Use affirmations that enhance your mental clarity, eloquence, and adaptability. Perform metaphysical workings that improve communication, whether it's for enhancing speaking abilities, writing skills, or clearer thinking.

Travel and Commerce: If you're embarking on a journey or a business venture, Wednesday is an ideal day to manifest safe travels and successful negotiations.

Intellectual Pursuits: Engage in rituals that support learning, studying, or any intellectual endeavors.

Offerings and Invocations: Present offerings to Mercury, Hermes, or Odin, such as items associated with them (e.g., coins for Mercury, runes for Odin). Recite prayers or invocations to these deities, asking for their guidance and blessings in your work.

Invoke the Frequency of Wednesday

Crystals & Herbs: Use crystals like agate, aventurine, or citrine, which resonate with Mercury's energy by carrying them with you throughout your day. Incorporate herbs such as lavender, fennel, or peppermint into your practices or make yourself some tea with these herbs. Burn incense like sandalwood or cinnamon to align with the day's energies and support your manifesting themes.

Dedicate time on Wednesdays for writing, studying, or engaging in intellectual discussions. Reach out to others for networking, social events, or meaningful conversations. By tuning into these correspondences and engaging in activities that resonate with Mercury's energy, you can enhance your manifesting and metaphysical workings on Wednesdays, while enhancing your power.

Invoke the Frequency of Thursday

In various traditions of astrology and magic, each day of the week is associated with specific planets and their corresponding energies. Thursday is traditionally linked to the planet Jupiter. Jupiter's energy is often associated with expansion, growth, abundance, luck, and wisdom. To align yourself with the frequency of Thursday and enhance your manifestations, you can focus on activities and practices that resonate with these themes during your manifesting. Jupiter is known for its expansive and generous nature. It's a good day for themes involving prosperity, growth, legal matters, higher learning, and spiritual wisdom.

Thursday Key

Planetary Influence: Jupiter
Attributes: Prosperity, growth, abundance, higher learning, spiritual wisdom, organization, optimism, prosperity, advancement
Frequency: 2560hz
Numerology association: No. 3
Element: Ether/Space
Colors: Blue, lilac, purple
Crystals/Minerals: Yellow sapphire, lapis lazuli, amethyst, turquoise
Metal: Tin
Herbs: Cinnamon, sage, bergamot, clove, dandelion, oak
Animals: Swan, centaur, unicorn
Chakra: Throat

Invoke the Frequency of Thursday

Color Correspondence: Wear or use colors associated with Jupiter, such as royal blue or purple, in your rituals or attire.

Crystals and Herbs: Utilize crystals like amethyst, sapphire, or lapis lazuli, and herbs like sage, clove, and cinnamon to enhance and invoke Jupiter's energy.

Deities and Spirits: Work with deities or spirits associated with Jupiter, such as Zeus, Thor, or Juno, depending on your tradition.

Meditation and Visualization: Meditate on themes of growth and abundance. Visualize the expansive and positive energy of Jupiter surrounding and infusing your intentions.

Affirmations and Intentions: Write or recite affirmations and set intentions related to prosperity, success, and wisdom.

Perform your magical workings on Thursday, ideally during the hour of Jupiter. In traditional planetary hours, the hour of Jupiter on Thursday would be the first hour after sunrise, but there are other Jupiter hours throughout the day. By aligning your metaphysical workings with the frequency of Thursday and the expansive, benevolent energy of Jupiter, you can enhance the effectiveness of your manifestations.

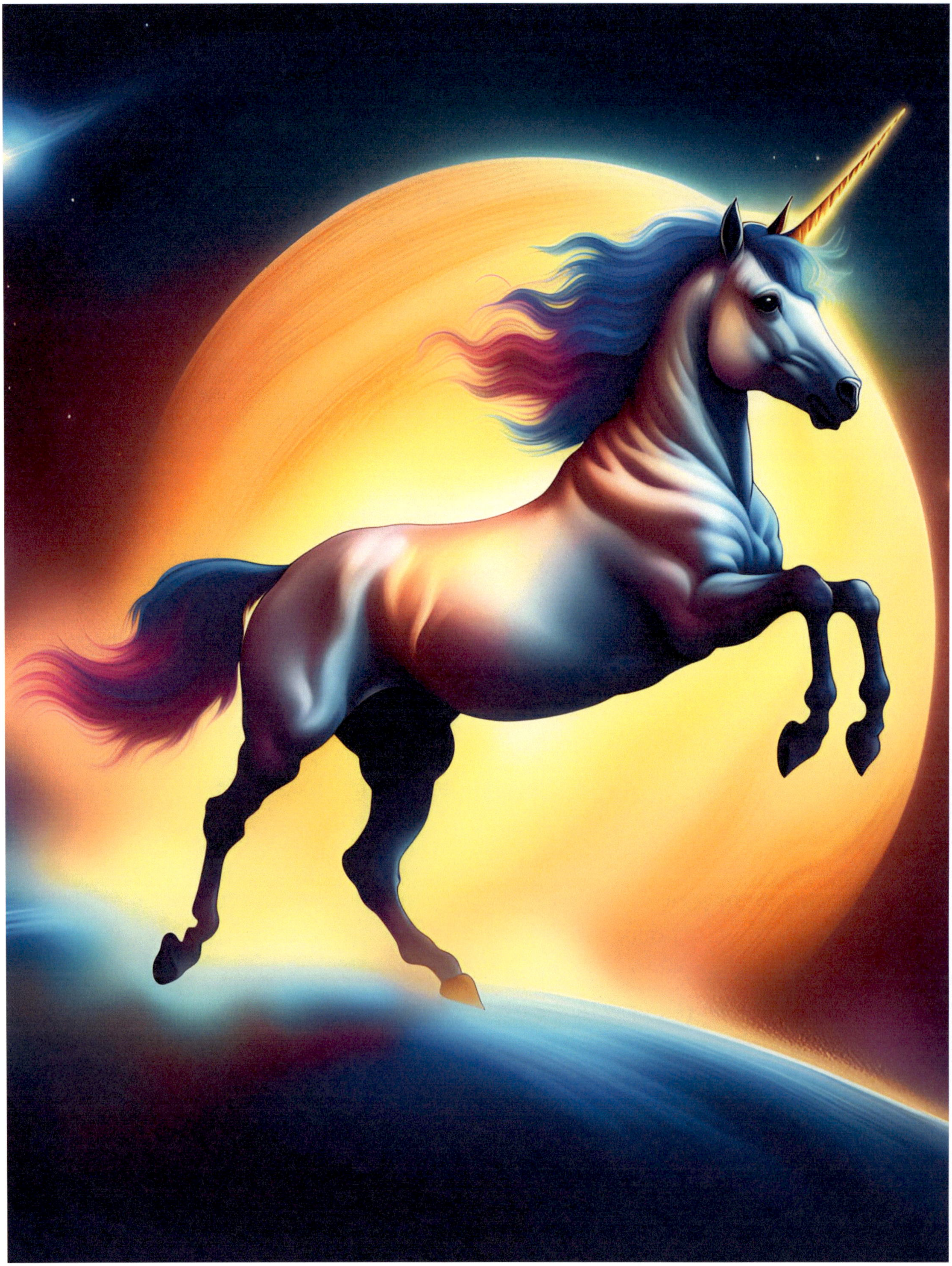

Invoke the Frequency of Friday

The concept of a frequency associated with a particular day, such as Friday, often ties into various spiritual, astrological, and ancient traditions. Here's an overview of the frequency of Friday and how one might align with it for enhancement of our manifestations. Friday is associated with the planet Venus. Venus governs love, beauty, pleasure, and harmony. Pamper yourself with activities that make you feel beautiful and cherished. By aligning your activities with the energies associated with Friday, you can enhance the effectiveness of your manifestations and bring more love, beauty, and harmony into your life.

Friday Key

Planetary Influence: Venus
Attributes: Love, beauty, pleasure, harmony, vitality, joy, artistic expression
Frequency: 480hz
Numerology association: No. 6
Element: Earth/Gaia
Colors: Green, pink, turquoise
Crystals/Minerals: Malachite, emerald, jade, sea salt
Metal: Copper
Herbs: Palo Santo, rose, violet, mint, thyme
Animals: Dove, rabbit, mermaid, dolphin, cat
Chakra: Heart

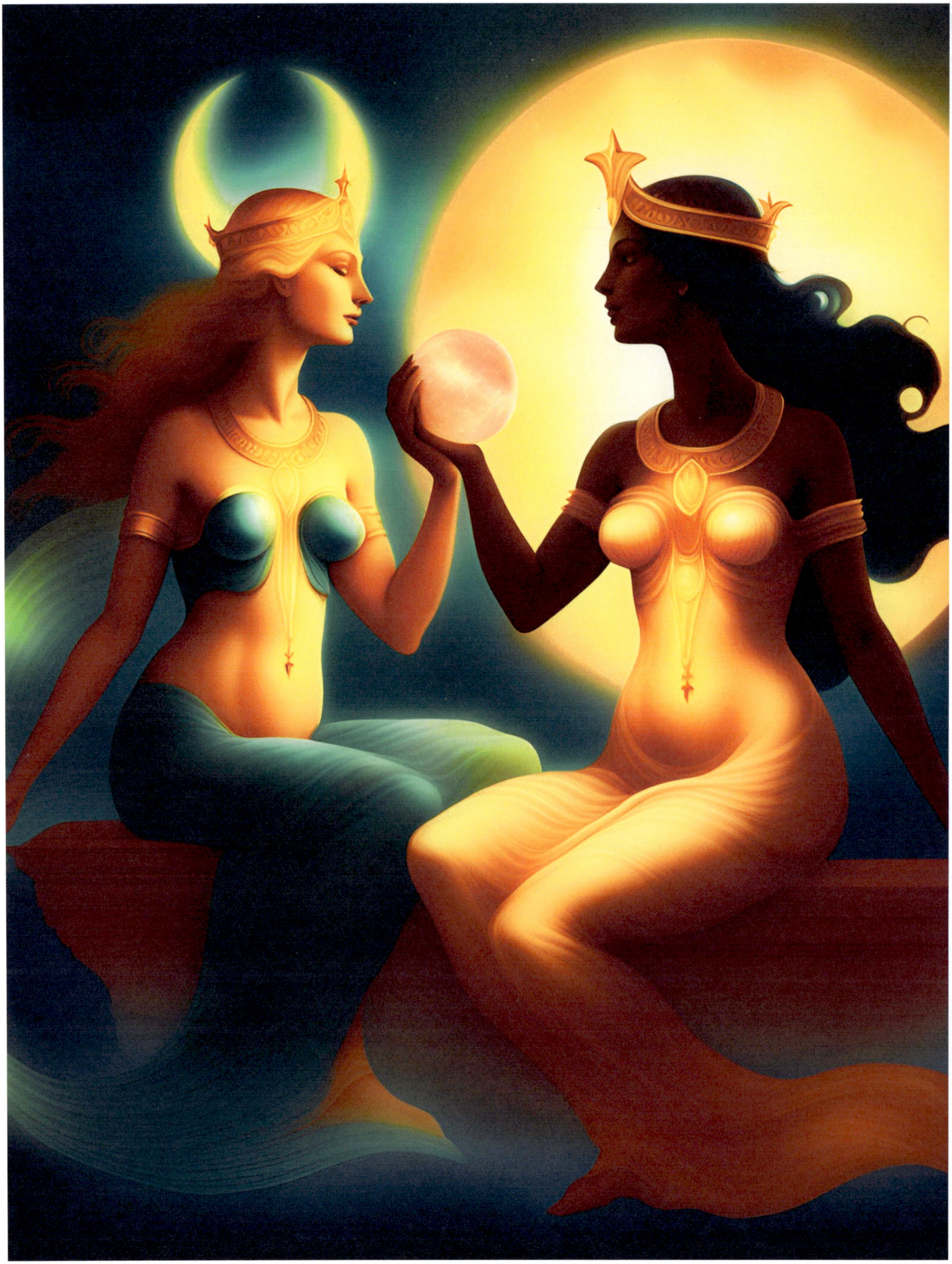

Invoke the Frequency of Friday

Mythological Associations: In Norse mythology, Friday is linked to the goddess Freyja (or Frigg), who is associated with love, beauty, and fertility. In Roman mythology, it is associated with Venus, the goddess of love and beauty.

Colors: Incorporate green and pink into your environment or attire. -

Crystals & Herbs: Use gemstones like rose quartz or emerald in your rituals. You may also Light pink or green candles.

Affirmations: Recite affirmations related to love, beauty, and harmony.

Meditation: Meditate on themes of love and balance, envisioning the energy of Venus enveloping you. Visualize your intentions blossoming with beauty and love. meditation on attracting love or strengthen relationships.

Engage in self-care rituals aimed at enhancing your beauty and self-love. Conduct metaphysical practices to manifest to financial abundance and prosperity. Engage in creative activities such as painting, writing, dancing or playing music. Spend time with loved ones or engage in social activities that bring joy and connection. Aligning your frequency to Friday will only assist you in your workings, making you more powerful and enhancing your manifestations.

Invoke the Frequency of Saturday

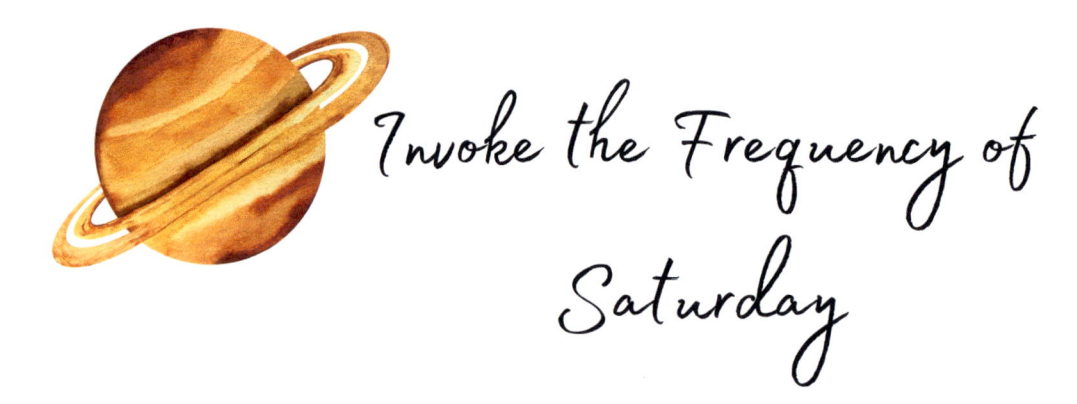

The concept of the "frequency of Saturday" is rooted in the idea that each day of the week has its own unique energy or vibration, often linked to the influences of celestial bodies and traditional planetary associations. Saturday is traditionally associated with Saturn, the planet named after the Roman god of agriculture, time, and endurance. Saturn's energy is often characterized by discipline, structure, responsibility, and the passage of time. Saturn's influence encourages focus on long-term goals, responsibilities, and disciplined efforts.

Saturday Key

Planetary Influence: Saturn
Attributes: Endurance, master of time, manifesting generator, forgiveness
Frequency: 5760hz
Numerology association: No. 8
Element: Earth
Colors: Black, indigo, grey, purple
Crystals/Minerals: Blue sapphire, diamond, jet, onyx
Metal: Lead
Herbs: Patchouli, cypress, juniper myrrh, lavendar
Animals: Bat, octopus, spider, goat, peacock
Chakra: Root

Invoke the Frequency of Saturday

Planning and Organization: Use Saturday to plan and organize your tasks, both mundane and magical. Create detailed plans and establish clear goals for your manifestations.

Cleansing and Protection: Perform practices that focus on protection, banishing negativity, and setting personal boundaries. This can involve using protective herbs, stones, or visualization techniques.

Grounding and Stability: Engage in grounding activities such as meditation, yoga, or spending time in nature to stabilize your energy.

Closure and completion are key themes. By aligning yourself with the disciplined and reflective energy of Saturday, you can enhance your manifestations bringing structure, protection, and a sense of closure to your practices. Take time for introspection, journaling, or meditation to reflect on your past week and set intentions for the future. Saturn represents the consistent hard work and patience you must pour into your manifestations. It's a good time to set or reinforce boundaries, evaluate limitations, and work within structures. Reflecting on past efforts and persevering through challenges is key.

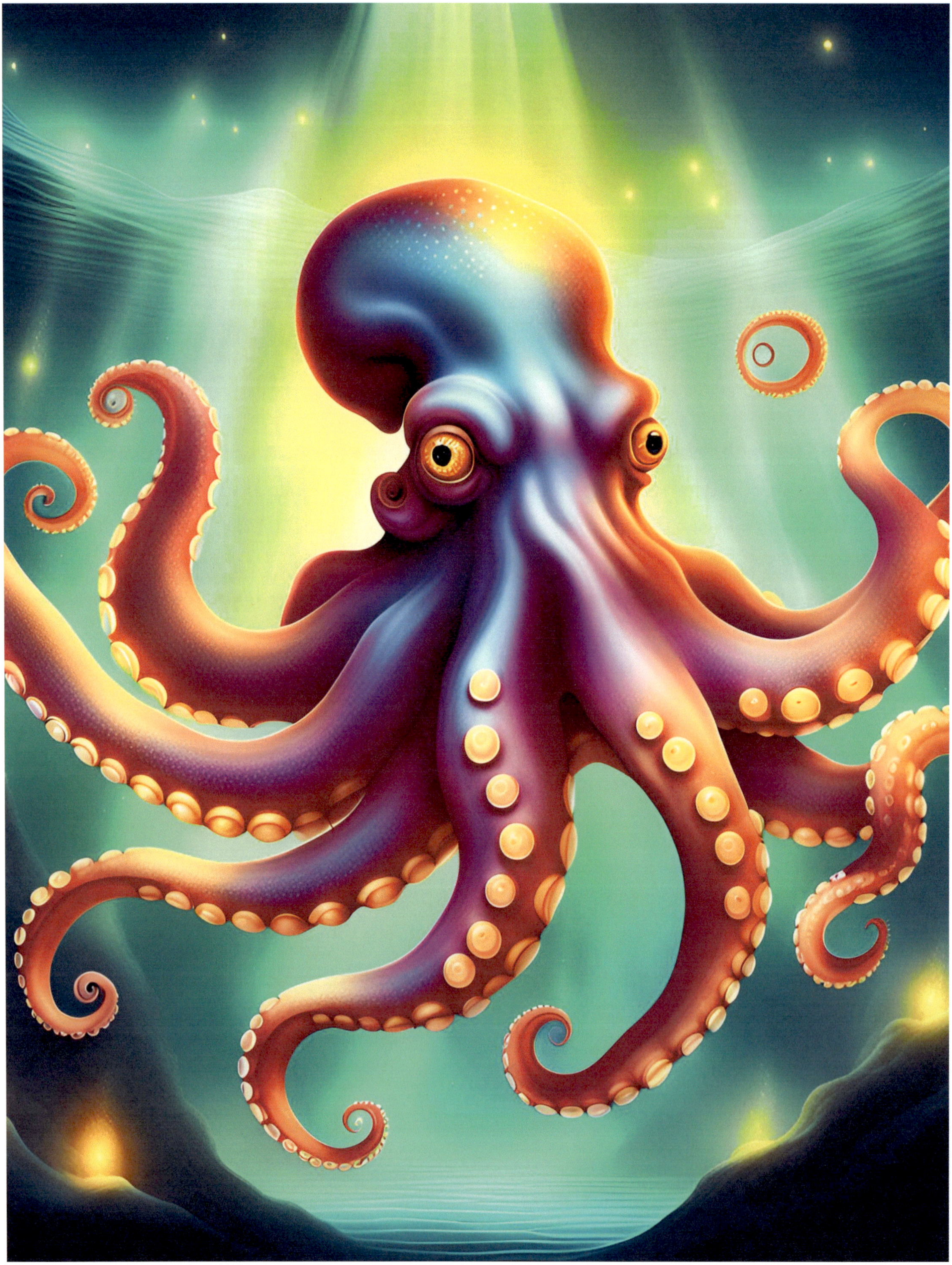

Invoke the Frequency of Sunday

The frequency of Sunday is associated with the Sun, which symbolizes vitality, success, illumination, and personal power. The energy of Sunday is vibrant, optimistic, and creative, making it an excellent day for activities that involve growth, enlightenment, and self-expression. The Sun represents life force, health, and vitality. It's a day to recharge and renew your energy. Sunday's energy supports endeavors that aim for success, achievement, and recognition. Focus on these themes in your manifestations.

Sunday Key

Planetary Influence: Sun
Attributes: Creativity, prophetic, future forward, illumination, clarity, growth, authority, leadership, optimism
Frequency: 1024hz
Numerology association: No. 1
Element: Fire
Colors: Gold, orange, red
Crystals/Minerals: Gold, ruby, tiger eye, citrine
Metal: Gold
Herbs: Calendula/marigold, sunflower, rosemary, copal, cedar, frankincense, angelica
Animals: Lion, tiger, panther, hawk, griffin
Chakra: Solar Plexus

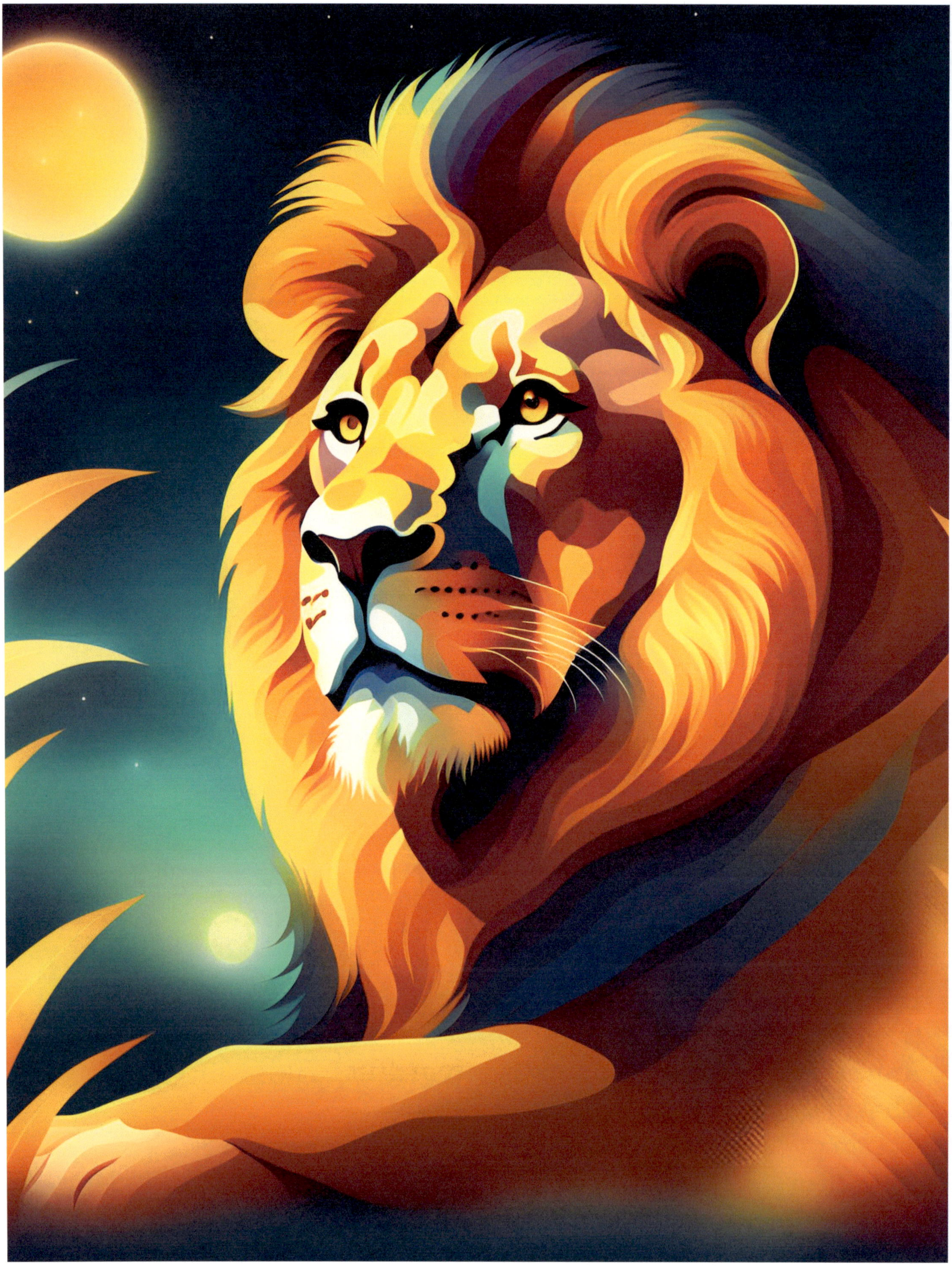

Invoke the Frequency of Sunday

Manifestation focus: Set new goals or revisit existing ones with a focus on success and achievement. Perform manifestation rituals to attract prosperity, success, and personal growth.

Meditation: Meditate on gaining clarity and insight into areas of your life that need illumination. Use visualization techniques to see your path clearly and understand your purpose.

It's a time for gaining insight, clarity, and understanding in various aspects of life. The Sun's influence enhances creativity, inspiration, and the expression of one's true self. Use Sunday to recharge your physical, mental, and spiritual energy. Engage in activities that make you feel alive and invigorated, such as exercise, spending time outdoors, or indulging in a hobby. Engage in creative endeavors such as writing, painting, or any artistic expression. Allow your creativity to flow freely, inspired by the vibrant energy of the Sun. Pamper yourself with self-care routines that enhance your well-being and confidence. Express your true self, whether through your appearance, actions, or words. By aligning yourself with the vibrant and illuminating energy of Sunday, you can boost your manifestations, fostering success, clarity, creativity, and personal power in your practices.

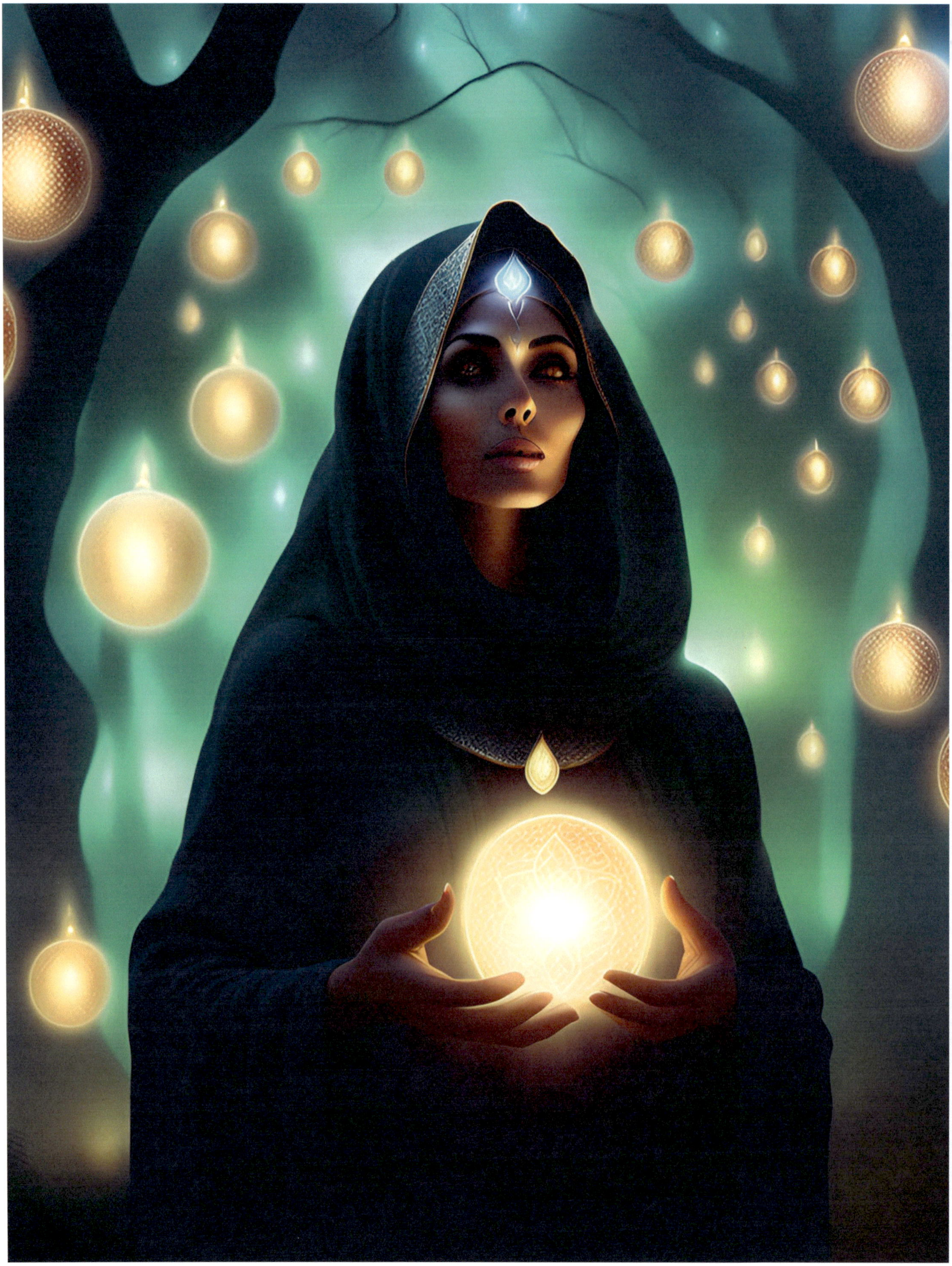

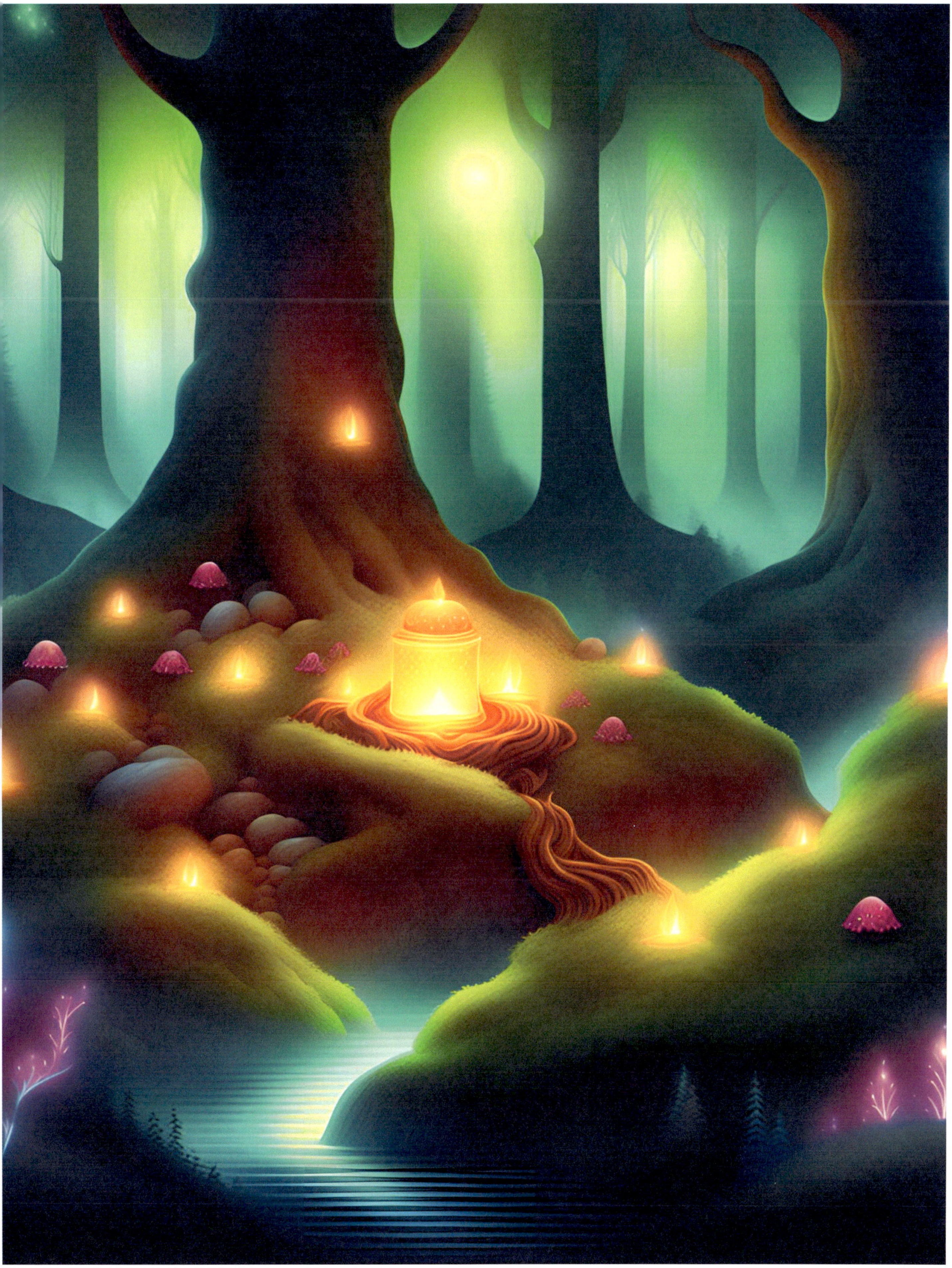

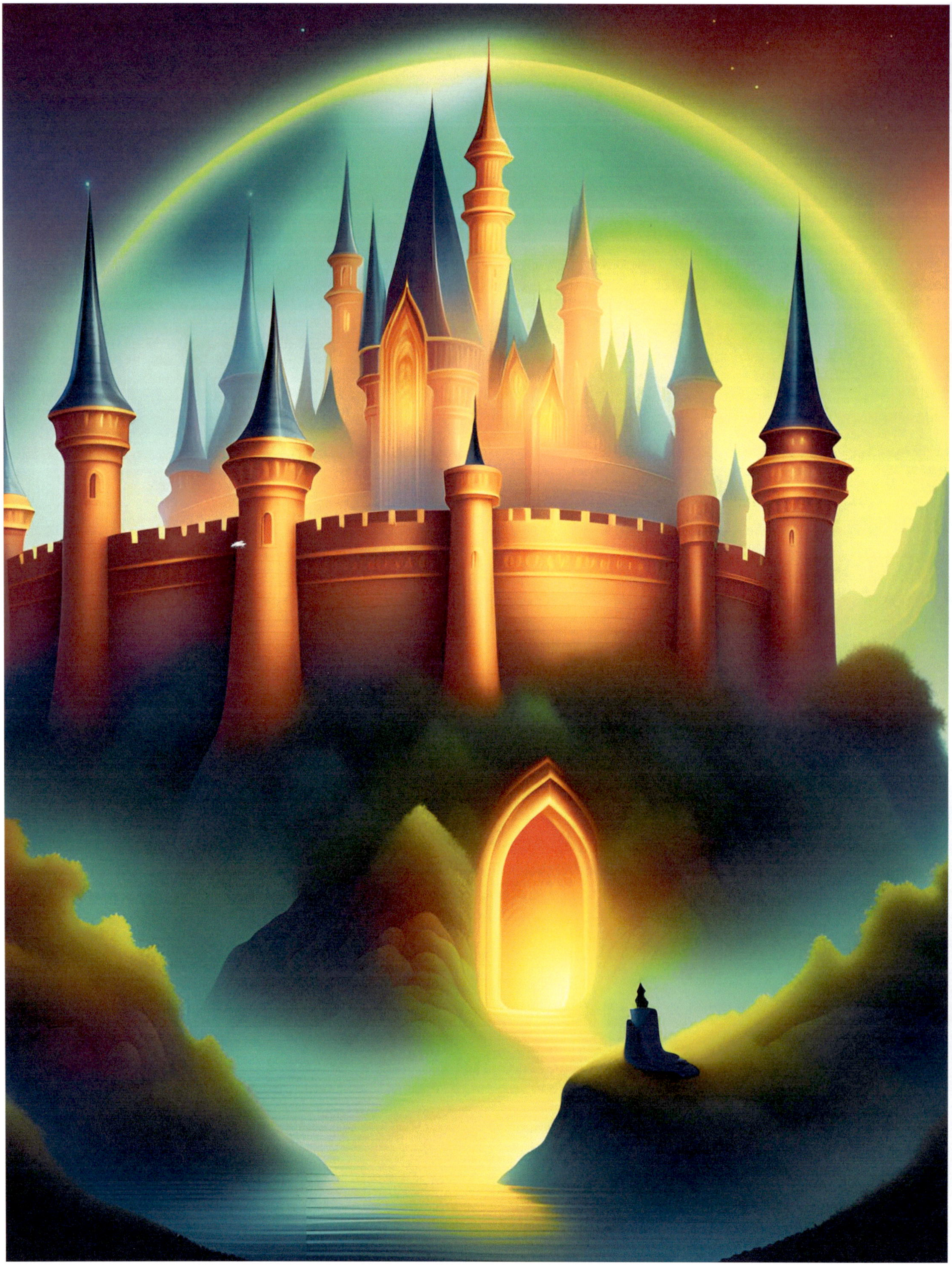

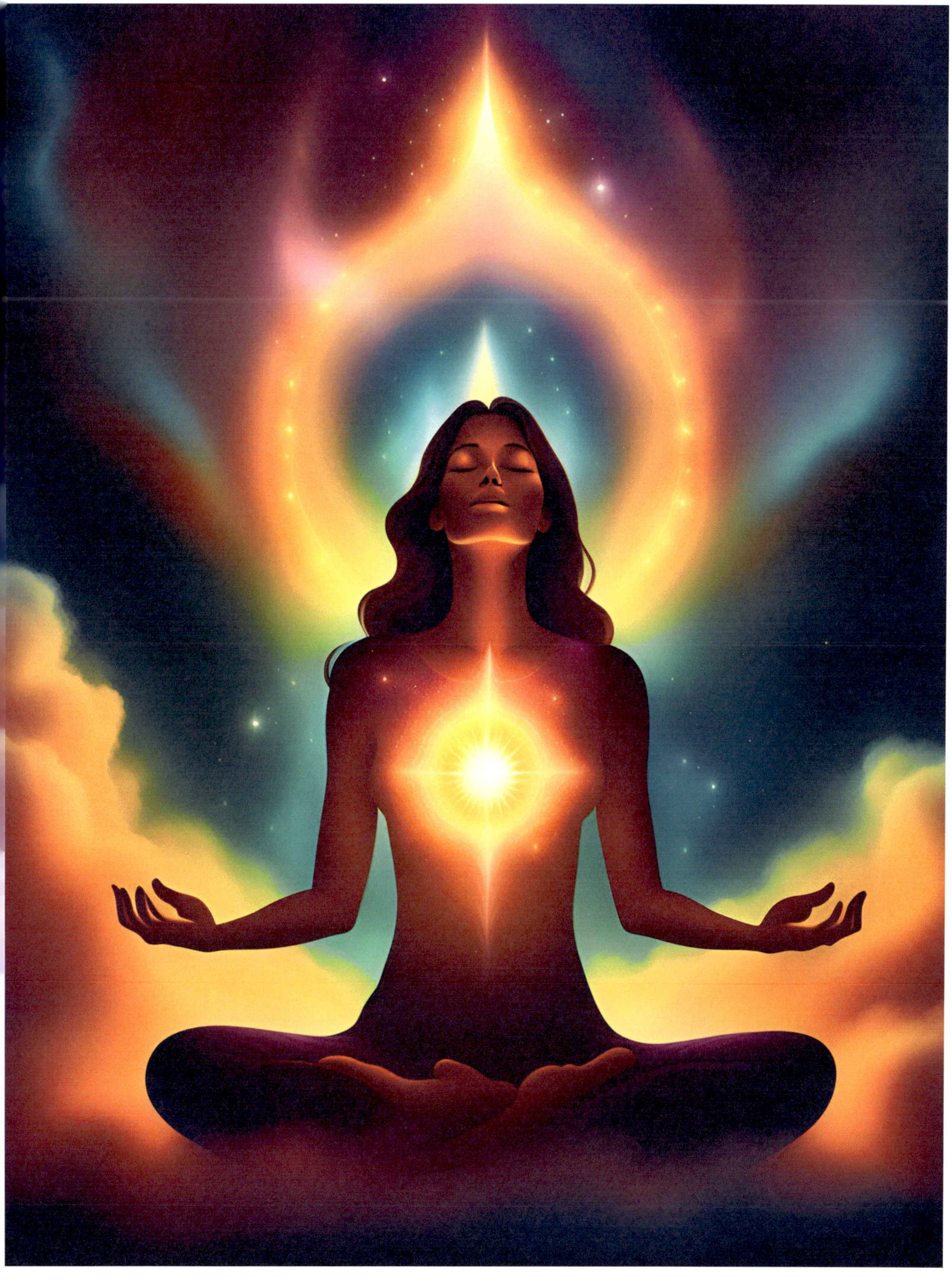

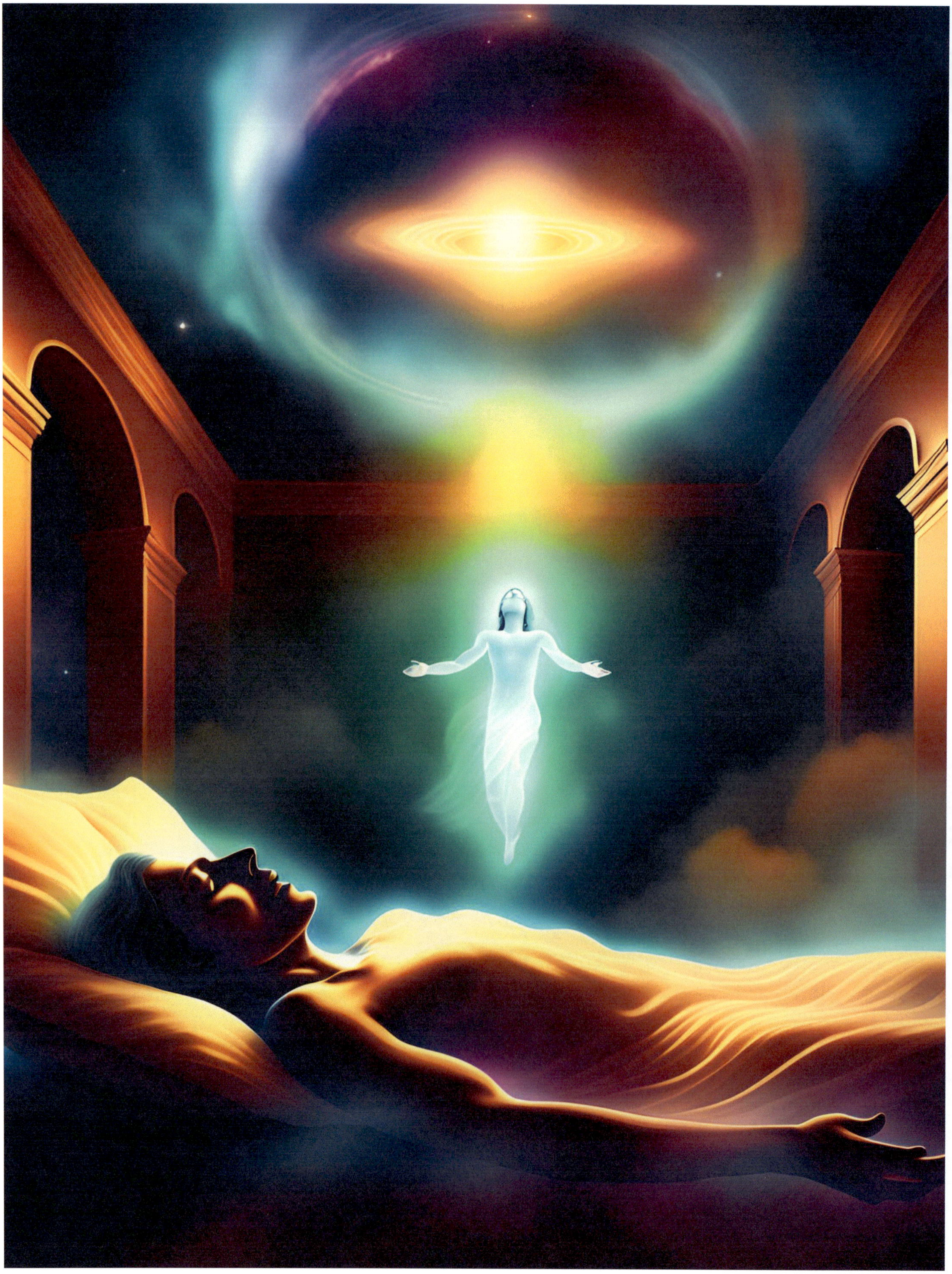

Vision Board

Professional Goals

(START DATE):   (END DATE):

○ _____
○ _____
○ _____
○ _____

Personal Goals

(START DATE):   (END DATE):

○ _____
○ _____
○ _____
○ _____

Financial Goals

(START DATE):   (END DATE):

○ _____
○ _____
○ _____
○ _____

⦿ TO START   ⊘ OK   ⊖ DELAY   ⊘ STUCK   ⊗ CANCEL

Vision Board

Health Goals

(Start Date):   *(End Date):*

- ○
- ○
- ○
- ○

Love Goals

(Start Date):   *(End Date):*

- ○
- ○
- ○
- ○

Spiritual Goals

(Start Date):   *(End Date):*

- ○
- ○
- ○
- ○

⦿ TO START   ⊘ OK   ⊖ DELAY   ⊘ STUCK   ⊗ CANCEL

Vision Board

Vision Board

Vision Board

Vision Board

Vision Board

Day 1
Journal

Date:

S | M | T | W | T | F | S

Water intake

💧 💧 💧 💧 💧 💧 💧 💧

Affirmations

○ _____
○ _____
○ _____
○ _____
○ _____
○ _____
○ _____
○ _____
○ _____

List of Gratitude

○ _____
○ _____
○ _____
○ _____
○ _____

Vision Board

What did I dream about last night?

_____
_____
_____
_____
_____
_____
_____
_____
_____
_____

Day 2
Journal

Date:

S | M | T | W | T | F | S

Water intake

○ ○ ○ ○ ○ ○ ○ ○

Affirmations
○ _____
○ _____
○ _____
○ _____
○ _____
○ _____
○ _____
○ _____
○ _____

List of Gratitude
○ _____
○ _____
○ _____
○ _____
○ _____

Vision Board

What did I dream about last night?
_____
_____
_____
_____
_____
_____
_____
_____
_____
_____
_____

Day 3
Journal

Date:

S | M | T | W | T | F | S

Water intake

○ ○ ○ ○ ○ ○ ○ ○

Affirmations

○ _____
○ _____
○ _____
○ _____
○ _____
○ _____
○ _____
○ _____
○ _____

List of Gratitude

○ _____
○ _____
○ _____
○ _____
○ _____

Vision Board

What did I dream about last night?

_____
_____
_____
_____
_____
_____
_____
_____
_____
_____

Day 4
Journal

Date:

S | M | T | W | T | F | S

Water intake

💧 💧 💧 💧 💧 💧 💧 💧

Affirmations

- _____
- _____
- _____
- _____
- _____
- _____
- _____
- _____
- _____

List of Gratitude

- _____
- _____
- _____
- _____
- _____

Vision Board

What did I dream about last night?

_____
_____
_____
_____
_____
_____
_____
_____
_____
_____

Day 5
Journal

Date:

S | M | T | W | T | F | S

Water intake

💧 💧 💧 💧 💧 💧 💧 💧

Affirmations

○ _____
○ _____
○ _____
○ _____
○ _____
○ _____
○ _____
○ _____
○ _____

List of Gratitude

○ _____
○ _____
○ _____
○ _____
○ _____

Vision Board

What did I dream about last night?

_____
_____
_____
_____
_____
_____
_____
_____
_____
_____

Day 6
Journal

Date:

S | M | T | W | T | F | S

Water intake

💧 💧 💧 💧 💧 💧 💧

Affirmations
- _____
- _____
- _____
- _____
- _____
- _____
- _____
- _____
- _____

List of Gratitude
- _____
- _____
- _____
- _____
- _____

Vision Board

What did I dream about last night?
_____
_____
_____
_____
_____
_____
_____
_____
_____
_____
_____

Day 7
Journal

Date:

S | M | T | W | T | F | S

Water intake

💧 💧 💧 💧 💧 💧 💧 💧

Affirmations
- _____
- _____
- _____
- _____
- _____
- _____
- _____
- _____
- _____

List of Gratitude
- _____
- _____
- _____
- _____
- _____

Vision Board

What did I dream about last night?
_____
_____
_____
_____
_____
_____
_____
_____
_____
_____

Day 8
Journal

Date:

S | M | T | W | T | F | S

Water intake

○ ○ ○ ○ ○ ○ ○ ○

Affirmations
- _____
- _____
- _____
- _____
- _____
- _____
- _____
- _____
- _____

List of Gratitude
- _____
- _____
- _____
- _____
- _____

Vision Board

What did I dream about last night?
_____
_____
_____
_____
_____
_____
_____
_____
_____
_____

Day 9
Journal

Date:

S | M | T | W | T | F | S

Water intake

💧 💧 💧 💧 💧 💧 💧 💧

Affirmations

- ○ _____
- ○ _____
- ○ _____
- ○ _____
- ○ _____
- ○ _____
- ○ _____
- ○ _____
- ○ _____

List of Gratitude

- ○ _____
- ○ _____
- ○ _____
- ○ _____
- ○ _____

Vision Board

What did I dream about last night?

_____
_____
_____
_____
_____
_____
_____
_____
_____
_____

Day 10
Journal

Date:

S | M | T | W | T | F | S

Water intake

💧 💧 💧 💧 💧 💧 💧

Affirmations
- _____
- _____
- _____
- _____
- _____
- _____
- _____
- _____
- _____

List of Gratitude
- _____
- _____
- _____
- _____
- _____

Vision Board

What did I dream about last night?
_____
_____
_____
_____
_____
_____
_____
_____
_____
_____

Day 11
Journal

Date:

S | M | T | W | T | F | S

Water intake

💧 💧 💧 💧 💧 💧 💧 💧

Affirmations

○ _____
○ _____
○ _____
○ _____
○ _____
○ _____
○ _____
○ _____
○ _____

List of Gratitude

○ _____
○ _____
○ _____
○ _____
○ _____

Vision Board

What did I dream about last night?

_____
_____
_____
_____
_____
_____
_____
_____
_____
_____

Day 12
Journal

Date:

S | M | T | W | T | F | S

Water intake

💧 💧 💧 💧 💧 💧 💧 💧

Affirmations
- _____
- _____
- _____
- _____
- _____
- _____
- _____
- _____
- _____

List of Gratitude
- _____
- _____
- _____
- _____
- _____

Vision Board

What did I dream about last night?
_____
_____
_____
_____
_____
_____
_____
_____
_____
_____

Day 13
Journal

Date:

S | M | T | W | T | F | S

Water intake

💧 💧 💧 💧 💧 💧 💧 💧

Affirmations
- _____
- _____
- _____
- _____
- _____
- _____
- _____
- _____
- _____

List of Gratitude
- _____
- _____
- _____
- _____
- _____

Vision Board

What did I dream about last night?
_____
_____
_____
_____
_____
_____
_____
_____
_____

Day 14
Journal

Date:

S | M | T | W | T | F | S

Water intake

○ ○ ○ ○ ○ ○ ○ ○

Affirmations
- _____
- _____
- _____
- _____
- _____
- _____
- _____
- _____
- _____

List of Gratitude
- _____
- _____
- _____
- _____
- _____

Vision Board

What did I dream about last night?
_____
_____
_____
_____
_____
_____
_____
_____
_____
_____

Day 15
Journal

Date:

S | M | T | W | T | F | S

Water intake

○ ○ ○ ○ ○ ○ ○ ○

Affirmations
○ _____
○ _____
○ _____
○ _____
○ _____
○ _____
○ _____
○ _____
○ _____

List of Gratitude
○ _____
○ _____
○ _____
○ _____
○ _____

Vision Board

What did I dream about last night?
_____
_____
_____
_____
_____
_____
_____
_____
_____
_____

Day 16
Journal

Date:

S | M | T | W | T | F | S

Water intake

💧 💧 💧 💧 💧 💧 💧 💧

Affirmations
- _____
- _____
- _____
- _____
- _____
- _____
- _____
- _____
- _____

List of Gratitude
- _____
- _____
- _____
- _____
- _____

Vision Board

What did I dream about last night?
_____
_____
_____
_____
_____
_____
_____
_____
_____
_____

Day 17
Journal

Date:

S | M | T | W | T | F | S

Water intake

💧 💧 💧 💧 💧 💧 💧 💧

Affirmations
- _____
- _____
- _____
- _____
- _____
- _____
- _____
- _____
- _____

List of Gratitude
- _____
- _____
- _____
- _____
- _____

Vision Board

What did I dream about last night?
_____
_____
_____
_____
_____
_____
_____
_____
_____

Day 18
Journal

Date:

S | M | T | W | T | F | S

Water intake

💧 💧 💧 💧 💧 💧 💧

Affirmations
- _____
- _____
- _____
- _____
- _____
- _____
- _____
- _____
- _____

List of Gratitude
- _____
- _____
- _____
- _____
- _____

Vision Board

What did I dream about last night?
_____
_____
_____
_____
_____
_____
_____
_____
_____
_____

Day 19
Journal

Date:

S | M | T | W | T | F | S

Water intake

○ ○ ○ ○ ○ ○ ○ ○

Affirmations

- _____
- _____
- _____
- _____
- _____
- _____
- _____
- _____
- _____

List of Gratitude

- _____
- _____
- _____
- _____
- _____

Vision Board

What did I dream about last night?

_____
_____
_____
_____
_____
_____
_____
_____
_____

Day 20
Journal

Date:

S | M | T | W | T | F | S

Water intake

💧 💧 💧 💧 💧 💧 💧 💧

Affirmations
- _____
- _____
- _____
- _____
- _____
- _____
- _____
- _____
- _____

List of Gratitude
- _____
- _____
- _____
- _____
- _____

Vision Board

What did I dream about last night?
_____
_____
_____
_____
_____
_____
_____
_____
_____
_____

Day 21
Journal

Date:

S | M | T | W | T | F | S

Water intake

💧 💧 💧 💧 💧 💧 💧 💧

Affirmations

○ _____
○ _____
○ _____
○ _____
○ _____
○ _____
○ _____
○ _____
○ _____

List of Gratitude

○ _____
○ _____
○ _____
○ _____
○ _____

Vision Board

What did I dream about last night?

_____
_____
_____
_____
_____
_____
_____
_____
_____

Day 22
Journal

Date:

S | M | T | W | T | F | S

Water intake

💧 💧 💧 💧 💧 💧 💧 💧

Affirmations
- _____
- _____
- _____
- _____
- _____
- _____
- _____
- _____
- _____

List of Gratitude
- _____
- _____
- _____
- _____
- _____

Vision Board

What did I dream about last night?
_____
_____
_____
_____
_____
_____
_____
_____
_____
_____

Day 23
Journal

Date:

S | M | T | W | T | F | S

Water intake

💧 💧 💧 💧 💧 💧 💧 💧

Affirmations
- _____
- _____
- _____
- _____
- _____
- _____
- _____
- _____
- _____

List of Gratitude
- _____
- _____
- _____
- _____
- _____

Vision Board

What did I dream about last night?
_____
_____
_____
_____
_____
_____
_____
_____
_____
_____

Day 24
Journal

Date:

S | M | T | W | T | F | S

Water intake

💧 💧 💧 💧 💧 💧 💧

Affirmations
- _____
- _____
- _____
- _____
- _____
- _____
- _____
- _____
- _____

List of Gratitude
- _____
- _____
- _____
- _____
- _____

Vision Board

What did I dream about last night?
_____
_____
_____
_____
_____
_____
_____
_____
_____
_____

Day 25
Journal

Date: _____

S | M | T | W | T | F | S

Water intake
💧 💧 💧 💧 💧 💧 💧 💧

Affirmations
○ _____
○ _____
○ _____
○ _____
○ _____
○ _____
○ _____
○ _____
○ _____

List of Gratitude
○ _____
○ _____
○ _____
○ _____
○ _____

Vision Board

What did I dream about last night?
_____
_____
_____
_____
_____
_____
_____
_____
_____
_____

Day 26
Journal

Date:

S | M | T | W | T | F | S

Water intake

💧 💧 💧 💧 💧 💧 💧 💧

Affirmations
- _____
- _____
- _____
- _____
- _____
- _____
- _____
- _____
- _____

List of Gratitude
- _____
- _____
- _____
- _____
- _____

Vision Board

What did I dream about last night?
_____
_____
_____
_____
_____
_____
_____
_____
_____
_____

Day 27
Journal

Date:

S | M | T | W | T | F | S

Water intake
○ ○ ○ ○ ○ ○ ○ ○

Affirmations
- _____
- _____
- _____
- _____
- _____
- _____
- _____
- _____
- _____
- _____

List of Gratitude
- _____
- _____
- _____
- _____
- _____

Vision Board

What did I dream about last night?
_____
_____
_____
_____
_____
_____
_____
_____
_____
_____

Day 28
Journal

Date:

S | M | T | W | T | F | S

Water intake

💧 💧 💧 💧 💧 💧 💧 💧

Affirmations
- _____
- _____
- _____
- _____
- _____
- _____
- _____
- _____
- _____

List of Gratitude
- _____
- _____
- _____
- _____
- _____

Vision Board

What did I dream about last night?
_____
_____
_____
_____
_____
_____
_____
_____
_____
_____

Day 29
Journal

Date:

S | M | T | W | T | F | S

Water intake
💧 💧 💧 💧 💧 💧 💧 💧

Affirmations
- _____
- _____
- _____
- _____
- _____
- _____
- _____
- _____
- _____

List of Gratitude
- _____
- _____
- _____
- _____
- _____

Vision Board

What did I dream about last night?
_____
_____
_____
_____
_____
_____
_____
_____
_____
_____

Day 30
Journal

Date:

S | M | T | W | T | F | S

Water intake

💧 💧 💧 💧 💧 💧 💧 💧

Affirmations
- _____
- _____
- _____
- _____
- _____
- _____
- _____
- _____
- _____

List of Gratitude
- _____
- _____
- _____
- _____
- _____

Vision Board

What did I dream about last night?
_____
_____
_____
_____
_____
_____
_____
_____
_____

Day 31
Journal

Date:

S | M | T | W | T | F | S

Water intake

💧 💧 💧 💧 💧 💧 💧

Affirmations
- _____
- _____
- _____
- _____
- _____
- _____
- _____
- _____
- _____

List of Gratitude
- _____
- _____
- _____
- _____
- _____

Vision Board

What did I dream about last night?
_____
_____
_____
_____
_____
_____
_____
_____
_____
_____

Day 32
Journal

Date:

S | M | T | W | T | F | S

Water intake

💧 💧 💧 💧 💧 💧 💧

Affirmations

- _____
- _____
- _____
- _____
- _____
- _____
- _____
- _____
- _____

List of Gratitude

- _____
- _____
- _____
- _____
- _____

Vision Board

What did I dream about last night?

_____
_____
_____
_____
_____
_____
_____
_____
_____
_____

Day 33
Journal

Date:

S | M | T | W | T | F | S

Water intake

◊ ◊ ◊ ◊ ◊ ◊ ◊ ◊

Affirmations

○ _____
○ _____
○ _____
○ _____
○ _____
○ _____
○ _____
○ _____
○ _____

List of Gratitude

○ _____
○ _____
○ _____
○ _____
○ _____

Vision Board

What did I dream about last night?

_____
_____
_____
_____
_____
_____
_____
_____
_____
_____

Day 34
Journal

Date:

S | M | T | W | T | F | S

Water intake

○ ○ ○ ○ ○ ○ ○ ○

Affirmations
- _____
- _____
- _____
- _____
- _____
- _____
- _____
- _____
- _____

List of Gratitude
- _____
- _____
- _____
- _____
- _____

Vision Board

What did I dream about last night?
_____
_____
_____
_____
_____
_____
_____
_____
_____

Day 35
Journal

Date:

S | M | T | W | T | F | S

Water intake

💧 💧 💧 💧 💧 💧 💧 💧

Affirmations

○ _____
○ _____
○ _____
○ _____
○ _____
○ _____
○ _____
○ _____
○ _____

List of Gratitude

○ _____
○ _____
○ _____
○ _____
○ _____

Vision Board

What did I dream about last night?

_____
_____
_____
_____
_____
_____
_____
_____
_____

Day 36
Journal

Date:

S | M | T | W | T | F | S

Water intake

💧 💧 💧 💧 💧 💧 💧

Affirmations
- _____
- _____
- _____
- _____
- _____
- _____
- _____
- _____
- _____

List of Gratitude
- _____
- _____
- _____
- _____
- _____

Vision Board

What did I dream about last night?
_____
_____
_____
_____
_____
_____
_____
_____
_____
_____

Day 37
Journal

Date:

S | M | T | W | T | F | S

Water intake
💧 💧 💧 💧 💧 💧 💧 💧

Affirmations
- _____
- _____
- _____
- _____
- _____
- _____
- _____
- _____
- _____

List of Gratitude
- _____
- _____
- _____
- _____
- _____

Vision Board

What did I dream about last night?
_____
_____
_____
_____
_____
_____
_____
_____
_____

Day 38
Journal

Date:

S | M | T | W | T | F | S

Water intake

💧 💧 💧 💧 💧 💧 💧 💧

Affirmations

- _____
- _____
- _____
- _____
- _____
- _____
- _____
- _____
- _____

List of Gratitude

- _____
- _____
- _____
- _____
- _____

Vision Board

What did I dream about last night?

_____
_____
_____
_____
_____
_____
_____
_____
_____
_____

Day 39
Journal

Date:

S | M | T | W | T | F | S

Water intake
💧 💧 💧 💧 💧 💧 💧 💧

Affirmations
○ _____
○ _____
○ _____
○ _____
○ _____
○ _____
○ _____
○ _____
○ _____

List of Gratitude
○ _____
○ _____
○ _____
○ _____
○ _____

Vision Board

What did I dream about last night?
_____
_____
_____
_____
_____
_____
_____
_____
_____

Day 40
Journal

Date:

S | M | T | W | T | F | S

Water intake

○ ○ ○ ○ ○ ○ ○ ○

Affirmations
- _____
- _____
- _____
- _____
- _____
- _____
- _____
- _____
- _____

List of Gratitude
- _____
- _____
- _____
- _____
- _____

Vision Board

What did I dream about last night?
_____
_____
_____
_____
_____
_____
_____
_____
_____
_____

Day 41
Journal

Date:

S | M | T | W | T | F | S

Water intake

💧 💧 💧 💧 💧 💧 💧

Affirmations
- _____
- _____
- _____
- _____
- _____
- _____
- _____
- _____
- _____

List of Gratitude
- _____
- _____
- _____
- _____
- _____

Vision Board

What did I dream about last night?
_____
_____
_____
_____
_____
_____
_____
_____
_____
_____

Day 42
Journal

Date:

S | M | T | W | T | F | S

Water intake

💧 💧 💧 💧 💧 💧 💧 💧

Affirmations
- _____
- _____
- _____
- _____
- _____
- _____
- _____
- _____
- _____

List of Gratitude
- _____
- _____
- _____
- _____
- _____

Vision Board

What did I dream about last night?
_____
_____
_____
_____
_____
_____
_____
_____
_____
_____

Day 43
Journal

Date:

S | M | T | W | T | F | S

Water intake

💧 💧 💧 💧 💧 💧 💧 💧

Affirmations
○ _____
○ _____
○ _____
○ _____
○ _____
○ _____
○ _____
○ _____
○ _____

List of Gratitude
○ _____
○ _____
○ _____
○ _____
○ _____

Vision Board

What did I dream about last night?
_____
_____
_____
_____
_____
_____
_____
_____
_____

Day 44
Journal

Date:

S | M | T | W | T | F | S

Water intake

💧 💧 💧 💧 💧 💧 💧

Affirmations

- _____
- _____
- _____
- _____
- _____
- _____
- _____
- _____
- _____

List of Gratitude

- _____
- _____
- _____
- _____
- _____

Vision Board

What did I dream about last night?
_____
_____
_____
_____
_____
_____
_____
_____
_____
_____

Day 45
Journal

Date:

S | M | T | W | T | F | S

Water intake

💧 💧 💧 💧 💧 💧 💧

Affirmations
○ _____
○ _____
○ _____
○ _____
○ _____
○ _____
○ _____
○ _____
○ _____

List of Gratitude
○ _____
○ _____
○ _____
○ _____
○ _____

Vision Board

What did I dream about last night?
_____
_____
_____
_____
_____
_____
_____
_____
_____
_____

Day 46
Journal

Date:

S | M | T | W | T | F | S

Water intake

◊ ◊ ◊ ◊ ◊ ◊ ◊ ◊

Affirmations

○ _____
○ _____
○ _____
○ _____
○ _____
○ _____
○ _____
○ _____
○ _____

List of Gratitude

○ _____
○ _____
○ _____
○ _____
○ _____

Vision Board

What did I dream about last night?

_____
_____
_____
_____
_____
_____
_____
_____
_____
_____

Day 47
Journal

Date:

S | M | T | W | T | F | S

Water intake

💧 💧 💧 💧 💧 💧 💧

Affirmations
- _____
- _____
- _____
- _____
- _____
- _____
- _____
- _____
- _____

List of Gratitude
- _____
- _____
- _____
- _____
- _____

Vision Board

What did I dream about last night?
_____
_____
_____
_____
_____
_____
_____
_____
_____

Day 48
Journal

Date:

S | M | T | W | T | F | S

Water intake

💧 💧 💧 💧 💧 💧 💧 💧

Affirmations
- _____
- _____
- _____
- _____
- _____
- _____
- _____
- _____
- _____

List of Gratitude
- _____
- _____
- _____
- _____
- _____

Vision Board

What did I dream about last night?
_____
_____
_____
_____
_____
_____
_____
_____
_____
_____

Day 49
Journal

Date:

S | M | T | W | T | F | S

Water intake

◊ ◊ ◊ ◊ ◊ ◊ ◊ ◊

Affirmations
- _____
- _____
- _____
- _____
- _____
- _____
- _____
- _____
- _____

List of Gratitude
- _____
- _____
- _____
- _____
- _____

Vision Board

What did I dream about last night?
_____
_____
_____
_____
_____
_____
_____
_____
_____
_____

Day 50
Journal

Date:

S | M | T | W | T | F | S

Water intake

💧 💧 💧 💧 💧 💧 💧 💧

Affirmations

- _____
- _____
- _____
- _____
- _____
- _____
- _____
- _____
- _____

List of Gratitude

- _____
- _____
- _____
- _____
- _____

Vision Board

What did I dream about last night?

_____
_____
_____
_____
_____
_____
_____
_____
_____
_____

Day 51
Journal

Date:

S | M | T | W | T | F | S

Water intake
💧 💧 💧 💧 💧 💧 💧 💧

Affirmations
- _____
- _____
- _____
- _____
- _____
- _____
- _____
- _____
- _____

List of Gratitude
- _____
- _____
- _____
- _____
- _____

Vision Board

What did I dream about last night?
_____
_____
_____
_____
_____
_____
_____
_____
_____

Day 52
Journal

Date:

S | M | T | W | T | F | S

Water intake

💧 💧 💧 💧 💧 💧 💧 💧

Affirmations
- _____
- _____
- _____
- _____
- _____
- _____
- _____
- _____
- _____

List of Gratitude
- _____
- _____
- _____
- _____
- _____

Vision Board

What did I dream about last night?
_____
_____
_____
_____
_____
_____
_____
_____
_____

Day 53
Journal

Date:

S | M | T | W | T | F | S

Water intake

💧 💧 💧 💧 💧 💧 💧 💧

Affirmations
- _____
- _____
- _____
- _____
- _____
- _____
- _____
- _____
- _____

List of Gratitude
- _____
- _____
- _____
- _____
- _____

Vision Board

What did I dream about last night?
_____
_____
_____
_____
_____
_____
_____
_____
_____

Day 54
Journal

Date:

S | M | T | W | T | F | S

Water intake

💧 💧 💧 💧 💧 💧 💧

Affirmations
- _____
- _____
- _____
- _____
- _____
- _____
- _____
- _____
- _____

List of Gratitude
- _____
- _____
- _____
- _____
- _____

Vision Board

What did I dream about last night?
_____
_____
_____
_____
_____
_____
_____
_____
_____
_____

Day 55
Journal

Date:

S | M | T | W | T | F | S

Water intake

💧 💧 💧 💧 💧 💧 💧 💧

Affirmations
- _____
- _____
- _____
- _____
- _____
- _____
- _____
- _____
- _____

List of Gratitude
- _____
- _____
- _____
- _____
- _____

Vision Board

What did I dream about last night?
_____
_____
_____
_____
_____
_____
_____
_____
_____
_____

Day 56
Journal

Date:

S | M | T | W | T | F | S

Water intake

○ ○ ○ ○ ○ ○ ○ ○

Affirmations
- _____
- _____
- _____
- _____
- _____
- _____
- _____
- _____
- _____

List of Gratitude
- _____
- _____
- _____
- _____
- _____

Vision Board

What did I dream about last night?
_____
_____
_____
_____
_____
_____
_____
_____
_____

Day 57
Journal

Date:

S | M | T | W | T | F | S

Water intake

💧 💧 💧 💧 💧 💧 💧 💧

Affirmations

○ _____
○ _____
○ _____
○ _____
○ _____
○ _____
○ _____
○ _____
○ _____

List of Gratitude

○ _____
○ _____
○ _____
○ _____
○ _____

Vision Board

What did I dream about last night?

_____
_____
_____
_____
_____
_____
_____
_____
_____
_____

Day 58
Journal

Date:

S | M | T | W | T | F | S

Water intake

💧 💧 💧 💧 💧 💧 💧 💧

Affirmations

-
-
-
-
-
-
-
-
-

List of Gratitude

-
-
-
-
-

Vision Board

What did I dream about last night?

_____
_____
_____
_____
_____
_____
_____
_____
_____
_____

Day 59
Journal

Date:

S | M | T | W | T | F | S

Water intake

💧 💧 💧 💧 💧 💧 💧

Affirmations

- _____
- _____
- _____
- _____
- _____
- _____
- _____
- _____
- _____

List of Gratitude

- _____
- _____
- _____
- _____
- _____

Vision Board

What did I dream about last night?

_____
_____
_____
_____
_____
_____
_____
_____
_____

Day 60
Journal

Date:

S | M | T | W | T | F | S

Water intake

○ ○ ○ ○ ○ ○ ○

Affirmations
- _____
- _____
- _____
- _____
- _____
- _____
- _____
- _____
- _____

List of Gratitude
- _____
- _____
- _____
- _____
- _____

Vision Board

What did I dream about last night?
_____
_____
_____
_____
_____
_____
_____
_____
_____

Day 61
Journal

Date:

S | M | T | W | T | F | S

Water intake

💧 💧 💧 💧 💧 💧 💧 💧

Affirmations
- _____
- _____
- _____
- _____
- _____
- _____
- _____
- _____
- _____

List of Gratitude
- _____
- _____
- _____
- _____
- _____

Vision Board

What did I dream about last night?
_____
_____
_____
_____
_____
_____
_____
_____
_____
_____

Day 62
Journal

Date:

S | M | T | W | T | F | S

Water intake

◊ ◊ ◊ ◊ ◊ ◊ ◊ ◊

Affirmations

○ _____
○ _____
○ _____
○ _____
○ _____
○ _____
○ _____
○ _____
○ _____

List of Gratitude

○ _____
○ _____
○ _____
○ _____
○ _____

Vision Board

What did I dream about last night?
_____
_____
_____
_____
_____
_____
_____
_____
_____
_____

Day 63

Journal

Date:

S | M | T | W | T | F | S

Water intake

💧 💧 💧 💧 💧 💧 💧

Affirmations

- _____
- _____
- _____
- _____
- _____
- _____
- _____
- _____
- _____

List of Gratitude

- _____
- _____
- _____
- _____
- _____

Vision Board

What did I dream about last night?

_____
_____
_____
_____
_____
_____
_____
_____
_____
_____

Day 64
Journal

Date:

S | M | T | W | T | F | S

Water intake

◊ ◊ ◊ ◊ ◊ ◊ ◊ ◊

Affirmations

○ _____
○ _____
○ _____
○ _____
○ _____
○ _____
○ _____
○ _____
○ _____

List of Gratitude

○ _____
○ _____
○ _____
○ _____
○ _____

Vision Board

What did I dream about last night?

_____
_____
_____
_____
_____
_____
_____
_____
_____
_____

Day 65
Journal

Date:

S | M | T | W | T | F | S

Water intake
○ ○ ○ ○ ○ ○ ○ ○

Affirmations
- _____
- _____
- _____
- _____
- _____
- _____
- _____
- _____
- _____

List of Gratitude
- _____
- _____
- _____
- _____
- _____

Vision Board

What did I dream about last night?
_____
_____
_____
_____
_____
_____
_____
_____
_____
_____

Day 66
Journal

Date:

S | M | T | W | T | F | S

Water intake

○ ○ ○ ○ ○ ○ ○ ○

Affirmations
-
-
-
-
-
-
-
-
-

List of Gratitude
-
-
-
-
-

Vision Board

What did I dream about last night?
_____
_____
_____
_____
_____
_____
_____
_____
_____

Made in the USA
Columbia, SC
22 March 2025